DISCARD

D1470474

Community Helpers
Crossing Guards
by Rebecca Pettiford

STOP

Bullfrog Books

Ideas for Parents and Teachers

Bullfrog Books let children practice reading informational text at the earliest reading levels. Repetition, familiar words, and photo labels support early readers.

Before Reading

- Discuss the cover photo. What does it tell them?

- Look at the picture glossary together. Read and discuss the words.

Read the Book

- "Walk" through the book and look at the photos. Let the child ask questions. Point out the photo labels.

- Read the book to the child, or have him or her read independently.

After Reading

- Prompt the child to think more. Ask: Have you ever seen a crossing guard? Did he or she help you cross a street?

Bullfrog Books are published by Jump!
5357 Penn Avenue South
Minneapolis, MN 55419
www.jumplibrary.com

Copyright © 2015 Jump! International copyright reserved in all countries. No part of this book may be reproduced in any form without written permission from the publisher.

Library of Congress Cataloging-in-Publication Data

Pettiford, Rebecca.
  Crossing guards / by Rebecca Pettiford.
     pages cm. — (Community helpers)
  Includes index.
  ISBN 978-1-62031-156-1 (hardcover) —
  ISBN 978-1-62496-243-1 (ebook)
  1. School crossing guards—Juvenile literature.
  I. Title.
  LB2865P48 2015
  371.7—dc23
                                          2014032161

Series Editor: Wendy Dieker
Series Designer: Ellen Huber
Book Designer: Anna Peterson
Photo Researcher: Casie Cook

Photo Credits: All photos by Shutterstock except: Alamy, 5, 10–11, 14–15, 18–19; Corbis, 3, 4, 12–13, 22, 23tl; Harry Hu/shutterstock.com, 17; iStockPhoto, 6–7; rSnapshotPhotos/shutterstock.com, 18; SuperStock, 16, 21, 23bl; Thinkstock, cover, 9.

Printed in the United States of America at Corporate Graphics in North Mankato, Minnesota.

RO452455742

Table of Contents

Crossing Guards at Work

Alex wants to be a crossing guard.

What do they do?

They help us
cross the street.

They keep us safe.

It's time for school.

Jo wears a bright vest.

She is easy to see.

9

crosswalk

Pat stands
in the crosswalk.

She has a big
stop sign.

Cars stop.

It is safe to cross.

Look out!

A car is coming!

Ray tells us to stay where we are.

STOP

raincoat

14

It's raining.

Mac is ready to work.

He has a raincoat.

It is bright.

We are going to the fair.

Officer John helps us cross the street.

17

Mae works in the city.

The street is busy!

She works hard to keep kids safe.

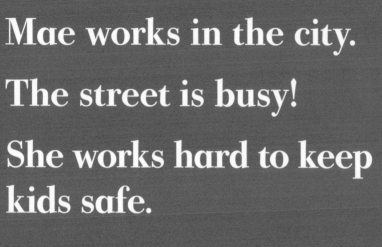

Crossing guards do good work!

In the Crosswalk

stop sign
A traffic sign that requires drivers to stop their vehicles.

pedestrian
Pedestrians are people who walk to get from place to place.

badge
Some crossing guards wear a badge to show they work at a school.

Picture Glossary

crosswalk
A painted area on the street marking a safe place for people to cross.

officer
A person in charge; sometimes police officers are crossing guards.

fair
An outdoor event, often with rides and games.

vest
A sleeveless top that is worn over a shirt.

Index

To Learn More

Learning more is as easy as 1, 2, 3.

1) Go to www.factsurfer.com

2) Enter "crossing guards" into the search box.

3) Click the "Surf" button to see a list of websites.

With factsurfer.com, finding more information is just a click away.